CERAMICS

HOW TO PAINT
CERAMICS

30 STEP-BY-STEP DECORATIVE PROJECTS

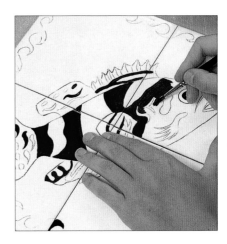

How to transform bowls, plates, cups, vases, jars and tiles into exquisite original pieces, with simple techniques and 300 inspirational photographs

Edited by SIMONA HILL

southwater

This edition is published by Southwater,
an imprint of Anness Publishing Ltd,
Blaby Road, Wigston, Leicestershire LE18 4SE;
info@anness.com

www.southwaterbooks.com; www.annesspublishing.com

If you like the images in this book and would like to
investigate using them for publishing, promotions
or advertising, please visit our website
www.practicalpictures.com for more information.

A CIP catalogue record for this book is available from the
British Library.

Publisher: Joanna Lorenz
Editorial Director: Helen Sudell
Editors: Simona Hill and Elizabeth Woodland
Designer: Nigel Partridge
Production Controller: Pirong Wang

Acknowledgements
The publisher would like to thank the following people for
designing projects in this book: Helen Baird for the Floral
Trinket Box, Spiral Vase and Mosaic Bedhead. Petra Boase
for the Mexican Folk Art Tiles. Marion Elliot for the Roman
Numeral Tiles, Byzantine Bird Tile, Pueblan Tiles,
Underwater Panel and Silver Decoupage Tiles. Mary
Fellows for the Alphabet Tiles, Cartoon Tiles and Autumn
Leaf Coffee Pot. Lucinda Ganderton for the Morning Sun
Face, Art Nouveau Tiles, Floral Tiles, Italianate Tiles,
Majolica Tile and William Morris Tiles. Lesley Harle for the
Heraldic Wall Plate, Low-relief Ceramic and Holly
Christmas Platter. Francesca Kaye for the Rosebud Tiles.
Izzy Moreau for the Stamped Spongeware and Maritime
Tile Mural. Helen Musselwhite for the Seashore Bathroom
Set, Patterned Lampbase, Fun Bunnies Tea Set and
Vegetable Storage Jars. Cleo Mussi for the Plant Pots.
Marie Perkins for the Sgraffito Fish Tiles, Citrus Fruit Bowl,
Kitchen Herb Jars and Sunflower Vase. Andrea Spencer for
the Seashore-style China. Isabel Stanley for the Leaf Motif
Cup and Saucer.

Notes
Protective clothing should be worn when performing
certain tasks described in this book. Wear rubber (latex)
gloves for grouting, and cleaning with hydrochloric acid;
wear leather gloves when breaking mosaic tesserae with a
hammer; wear goggles when breaking tesserae with a
hammer using tile nippers and cleaning with hydrochloric
acid; wear a face mask when sanding, cleaning with
hydrochloric acid,and working with the following:
powdered grout, cement sprays (such as adhesive or
varnish) and lead came.

Publisher's Note
Although the advice and information in this book are
believed to be accurate and true at the time of going to
press, neither the authors nor the publisher can accept any
legal responsibility or liability for any errors or omissions
that may have been made nor for any inaccuracies nor for
any loss, harm or injury that comes about from following
instructions or advice in this book.

Contents

Introduction

Decorating ceramics and tiles with paint is easy to do and it is a wonderful way to transform plain china. Old bowls, cups and plates, jars, and white or

coloured tiles, can be given a new lease of life with a splash of paint, as well as brightening up your home. Likewise, making a ceramic mosaic provides a fun way of using up old and unwanted crockery and tiles and you create a unique decorative item for your home.

As well as explaining and illustrating all the different techniques of painting on china and making mosaics, this book contains over 30 step-by-step projects ranging from simple to complex and from small to large. You can begin with the sponged snowflake plate or cartoon tiles and progress on to the more challenging floral trinket box. The symbol 🖌 indicates that a project is relatively straightforward to do and one a complete beginner could tackle with ease. Projects with the symbol 🖌🖌🖌🖌 indicate that an advanced level of skill

and knowledge is required to complete the work. You do not need to be proficient at drawing to be able to decorate ceramics, and to inspire you, there is a wide range of templates included at the back of the book which you can photocopy and enlarge to

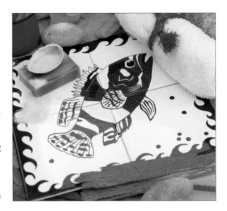

the size required. Simple painted motifs, such as shells, stars or sunflowers, add colour and a personal stamp to your china, and patterns such as stripes or dots can look very effective around the rim of a plate or cup. Once you are more confident, try smudging or overlapping colours to add charm to the hand-painted effect.

Before you launch straight into a project, however, practise on an old piece of china or a white tile, just to get a feel for the brush and the paint technique, and to see that your chosen colour looks right. The same goes for ceramic mosaic: arrange your tesserae in position before sticking them down, to make sure that the colours work well together and to check that you have enough pieces to complete your design.

With so many fun and creative projects to choose from and clear step-by-step instructions to follow, you will quickly become proficient at painting on ceramics and making mosaics, and produce professional results you can be proud of.

Decorating

Ceramics

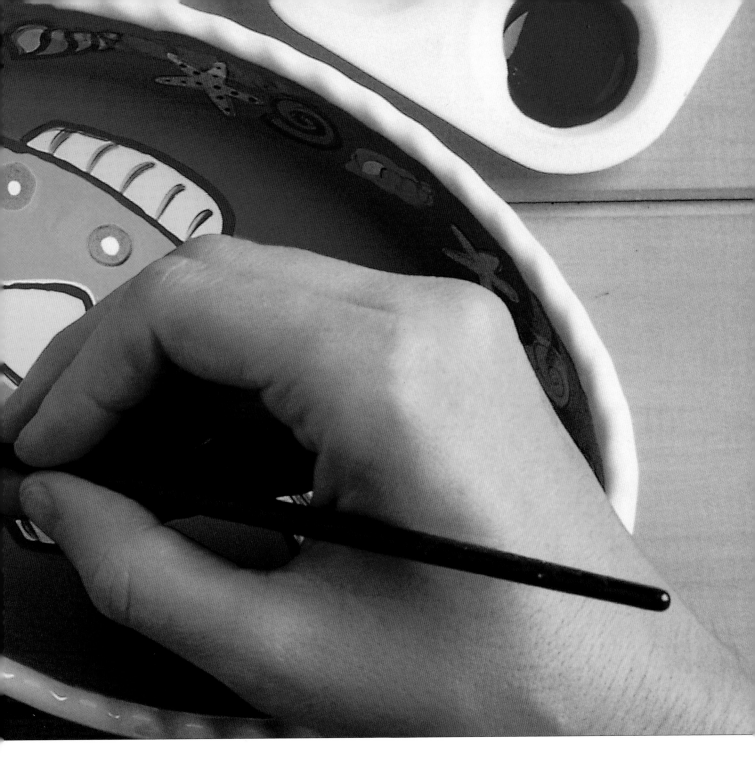

You do not need to be an expert artist or have trained drawing skills to paint

beautiful designs on ceramics. All you need is the enthusiasm to have a go,

and a design or a colour palette that will inspire you to follow through your

idea. So even if you think you can't draw, there are templates to trace that

take the hard work out of designing and will make colouring your design as

easy as painting by numbers.

A variety of materials is needed for painting on ceramics, all of which are available from craft stores. Many items can be improvised, but some materials, such as paints, have to be specially purchased.

Materials

surfaces that may come in contact with foodstuffs or the mouth such as serving plates, bowls and cups.

Solvent-based ceramic paints

These come in a huge range of colours and lend themselves well to varied painting styles such as wash effects. White spirit (paint thinner) can be used to dilute the paint and to clean paintbrushes after use. Solvent-based paints take approximately 24 hours to dry. They can then be varnished to protect the finish.

Water-based ceramic paints

Sold under various trade names and specially made for painting glazed ceramics, these paints are available in a range of colours. They produce a strong, opaque, flat colour and can be diluted with water. Wash paintbrushes in warm water immediately after painting. Water-based paints dry in around 3 hours; do not attempt to bake them until they are completely dry or the colour may bubble. Baking the painted item will make the colour durable enough for a dishwasher. Put the item in a cold oven and do not remove it after baking until it has completely cooled. Always follow the paint manufacturer's instructions for the temperature and baking time, and do a test first as over-firing can turn the colour slightly brown.

Enamel paints

These paints are not made exclusively for china and ceramics. They are available in a range of colours and dry to a hard and durable finish. They contain lead and should only ever be used for decorative purposes and not on items that will contain food.

Masking fluid

Watercolour art masking fluid is used to mask off areas of the design while colour is applied to the surrounding

area. Apply to a clean, dry surface. Always allow the masking fluid to dry before filling in the design with paint.

Polyurethane varnish and glazes

Apply varnish evenly, using a large, flat brush and stroking in one direction over the ceramic. The more coats you apply, the more durable and washable the surface, but keep each of the coats thin, allowing a minimum of 4 hours' drying time between coats. Polyurethane varnish is unsuitable for

No expensive specialist equipment is required for painting ceramics. In fact, you probably already have much of the equipment needed among your normal household supplies.

Equipment

Paintbrushes
Use a fine brush for details, and a broad soft brush for covering larger areas.

Paint palette
Use to mix and hold paints.

Pencils and pens
A hard pencil is good for transferring designs; a soft for direct marking.

Printing blocks
Use for printing repeated patterns.

Ruler or straightedge
Plastic rules measure adequately. For cutting, metal ones are better.

Scissors
Use to cut paper patterns.

Self-healing cutting mat
This protects the work surface when cutting paper with a craft knife.

Stencil cardboard
This is manila card (cardboard) water-proofed with linseed oil.

Tracing paper
Use with carbon paper to transfer designs on to the object to be painted.

White spirit (paint thinner)
Use to clean brushes, to remove paint mistakes and to thin paint.

Carbon paper
Use to transfer designs on to ceramic. Place it carbon side down, on the object. Stick the image drawn on tracing paper on top. Draw over the image to transfer it to the ceramic.

Clear adhesive tape
Use for sticking designs to ceramic.

Craft knife
Use with a metal ruler and cutting mat for cutting papers and cardboard.

Masking film (frisket paper)
This self-adhesive transparent paper has a waxed paper backing, which peels away. Use it to mask out areas you want to keep blank.

Masking tape
Use to hold stencils in place and to mask off areas of ceramic.

Natural and synthetic sponges
Use to create paint effects for anything from an even to a textured finish.

The projects in this chapter do not require any specialist skills but it is worth practising a few painting techniques before you start. The tips suggested below will prove useful as you work through the ideas.

Techniques

Cleaning china

Before painting any white china, always clean it thoroughly to remove any invisible traces of dirt or grease. Effective cleaning agents are cleaning fluid, turpentine, methylated spirit (methyl alcohol), lighter fuel or white spirit (paint thinner). Keep these materials away from naked flames.

Safe drinking vessels

To ensure that there is no possibility of any paint being swallowed when drinking from a mug or glass, adapt designs so that any colour you paint is at least 3cm/1¼in below the rim of drinking vessels. Otherwise the piece should be fired in a kiln.

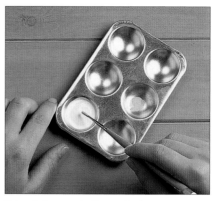

Working with paints

Paints suitable for applying to china are available in water or oil-based types. When mixing up a shade of your own, remember that the two types of paint cannot be intermixed. Always thoroughly clean brushes as directed by the paint manufacturer.

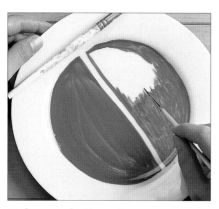

Using paintbrushes

Always use an appropriately sized paintbrush for the task in hand. Larger areas should always be painted with a large brush using bold strokes, while small, fine brushes are best for all detailed work.

Watery effects

You can achieve a watery effect in oil-based colours by diluting paints with white spirit (paint thinner). Water-based paints can be diluted by adding water.

Creating white lines

If you want to leave thin lines of china showing through areas of colour, paint them in first with masking fluid. This can be gently peeled off when the paint is dry to reveal the white china beneath. Use an instrument with a sharp point such as a craft knife or compass to lift off the dried masking fluid.

Using masking fluid

Add a drop of water-based paint to masking fluid before use when you are working on plain white china. This will help you to see where the masking fluid has been applied, enabling you to wipe it off easily when you are ready to do so.

Preparing a sponge

Use a craft knife to cut cubes of sponge for sponging paint. Hold the sponge taut as you slice down into it to make cutting easier and the lines straight. Keep several sponge cubes to hand when sponging as you may need to change them frequently.

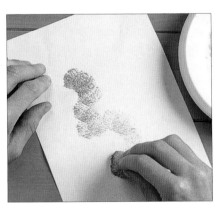

Testing a sponge

Before sponging on to your china after loading the sponge with paint, test the print on a scrap piece of paper. The first print or two will be too saturated with paint to achieve a pleasing effect.

Sponging variations

A stencilled design can be made more interesting by varying the density of the sponging within the image or by adding more than one colour. Allow the first coat of paint to dry partially before the application of the second.

Printing blocks

Test the print on scrap paper before you print on the china. When using printing blocks, roll the block lightly on to the surface to ensure you get a good, even print.

Straight lines

Masking tape is useful for painting straight edges, stripes and even checks and squares. Just stick it down to mark out areas you do not want painted and apply the paint. Remove the tape before the paint is completely dry; straight lines of paint will be left.

Removing masking tape or film

When using masking tape or film (frisket paper), it is better to remove it before the paint is completely dry as this will give a cleaner edge to the pattern beneath.

Tracing

Use tracing paper and a soft pencil to transfer designs directly on to china. First trace the template or the design you wish to use, then fix the tracing paper to the china with pieces of masking tape. Rub over the traced design with a soft pencil to transfer.

Removing guide markings

Pencil or pen guide marks on the china are easy to wipe off once the paint is completely dry or has been baked. Use a damp paper towel or cloth and take care not to rub the paint too hard.

Testing new techniques

Always test out a technique that you have not tried before. Apply the new technique to a spare piece of china, which can be cleaned up easily, rather than to a piece you are already in the process of decorating.

Removing unwanted paint

Use a pencil eraser or cotton buds (swabs) to tidy up a design or to wipe off small areas of unwanted paint. For larger areas use a damp paper towel or cloth. Allow the cleaned area to dry before repainting.

Preparing a stencil A stencil is a thin sheet with a decorative pattern cut out, through which paint is applied. This can be used to repeat the pattern on a chosen surface. Try designing and making your own.

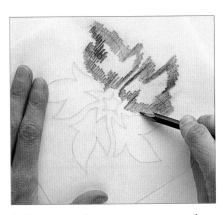

1 To transfer a template on to a piece of stencil cardboard, place a piece of tracing paper over the design, and draw over it with a hard pencil.

2 Turn over the tracing paper, and on the back of the design rub over the lines you have drawn with a pencil.

3 Turn the tracing paper back to the right side and place on top of a sheet of stencil cardboard. Draw over the original lines with a hard pencil.

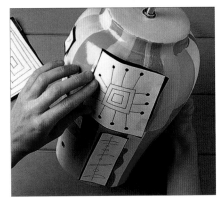

4 To cut out the stencil, place the stencil on to a cutting mat or piece of thick cardboard and tape in place. Use a craft knife for cutting.

5 To transfer a detailed design using carbon paper, place the stencil over a piece of carbon paper, carbon side down. Attach the carbon paper to the china piece with masking tape. Use a soft pencil to trace the shape lightly on to the china.

Stencilling offers a quick and easy method of decorating china. The simple shapes of these limes look terrific adorning a fruit bowl. Choose just two or three bold colours for maximum effect.

Citrus Fruit Bowl

You will need
soft pencil
tracing paper
masking tape
stencil cardboard
self-healing cutting mat
craft knife
plain fruit bowl
cleaning fluid
cloth
yellow chinagraph pencil
water-based ceramic paints: citrus green, mid-green, dark green and yellow
paint palette
artist's paintbrushes
acrylic varnish (optional)

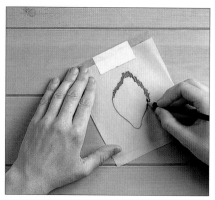

1 Draw a freehand lime shape on to tracing paper. Using masking tape to hold the tracing paper securely in place, transfer the lime outline to a piece of stencil cardboard. Working on a self-healing cutting mat, carefully cut all around the shape of the lime using a craft knife with a sharp blade.

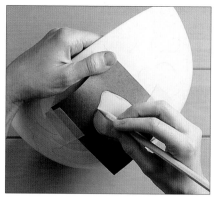

2 Clean a plain fruit bowl. Attach the stencil to the bowl using masking tape. Draw inside the stencil outline on to the bowl using a yellow chinagraph pencil. Repeat to draw several limes all over the bowl.

3 Fill in all the lime shapes with citrus green paint using an artist's paintbrush. Allow the paint to dry completely. Add highlights to each of the fruits using the mid-green paint and allow the paint to dry thoroughly as before.

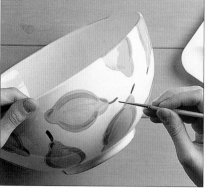

4 Paint a stalk at the end of each lime shape in the dark green paint. Allow to dry. Paint the background all over the outside of the bowl yellow, leaving a thin white outline around each of the lime shapes to help them stand out.

5 To complete the bowl, either use a clean brush to apply a coat of acrylic varnish over the painted section, or bake the bowl in the oven, following the paint manufacturer's instructions.

Add colour to a plain white dinner service by embellishing it with ceramic paints. You can use the motifs to create different designs for each place setting, or make the whole set the same.

Seashore-style China

You will need

tracing paper

pencil

scissors

china plates and soup bowls

cloth

cleaning fluid

ruler

carbon paper

masking tape

blue solvent-based ceramic paint

fine artist's paintbrush

cloth

1 Copy the templates from the back of the book on to tracing paper. Cut out the shapes with scissors. Clean the plate and bowl thoroughly with a cloth and cleaning fluid.

2 To decorate a plate, find and mark the middle with a ruler and pencil. Divide the plate into eight equal parts and lightly mark up the eight sections in pencil.

3 If you make plenty of copies of each design, you can use your templates to experiment with various design options.

4 Cut a piece of carbon paper into small pieces to fit your templates.

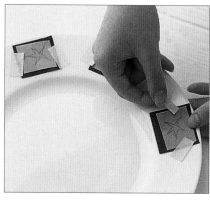

5 Place the carbon paper under the template designs on the plate and stick them down firmly with masking tape to secure.

6 Trace around the template outlines with a sharp pencil, then remove the masking tape, templates and carbon paper to reveal the design.

7 Paint in the shapes carefully using blue solvent-based ceramic paint. Leave to dry thoroughly.

8 Mark, trace and paint the design in the centre of the soup bowl. Add small dots on the handles of the bowl. Leave to dry. Remove the pencil lines.

Ceramics with low-relief decorative motifs are ideal for painting. Like children's colouring books, the shapes are all set out ready to colour in and, as there are no clearly defined outlines, mistakes will go unnoticed.

Low-relief Ceramic

You will need

clean, white glazed pitcher with a low-relief fruit motif

medium and fine artist's paintbrushes

solvent-based ceramic paints: acid yellow, golden yellow, light green, medium green and dark green

polyurethane varnish or glaze

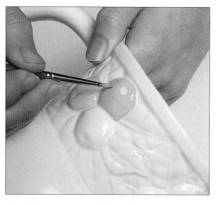

1 Paint some of the lemons on the pitcher acid yellow. Vary them so that one group has two acid yellow lemons, the next group one, and so on. Leave a narrow white line around each lemon, and leave the seed cases and the small circles at the base of the fruit white. Allow to dry.

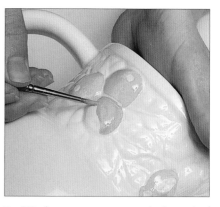

2 Work your way around the relief pattern at the top of the pitcher, painting the remaining fruit a rich golden yellow. Using two yellows for the fruit creates a sense of depth and variety. Once again, leave a narrow white line around each fruit, and leave the paint to dry.

3 Starting with light green, paint roughly a third of the leaves, evenly spaced apart if possible, but don't worry about being too exact. Leave the central midrib of each leaf and a narrow line around each leaf white. Allow to dry. Paint the small circles.

4 Paint a third of the leaves medium green, spacing them evenly. Paint a narrow green line around the base of the pitcher and leave to dry. Paint the remaining leaves dark green and leave to dry.

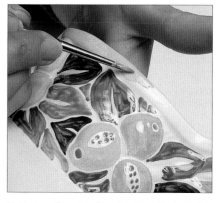

5 Paint the rim (or the handle) of the pitcher in acid yellow, leaving a narrow white line at the lower edge. Once the paint is dry, varnish the pitcher with polyurethane varnish or the glaze provided specially by the ceramic paint manufacturer for this purpose.

Imagine the effect produced by a whole set of this delightful sponge-ware design, set out on your kitchen shelves. Painting your own mugs in this lovely decorative style is an easy way of transforming plain china.

Stamped Spongeware

You will need

ballpoint pen

cellulose kitchen sponge

scissors

all-purpose glue

corrugated cardboard

ceramic paints: dark blue and dark green

paint palette

kitchen paper

clean, white china mugs

masking tape

craft knife

fine black felt-tipped pen

stencil brush or small cosmetic sponge

1 Draw a crab on the sponge. Cut out and glue to the corrugated cardboard. Trim as close as possible. Press the sponge into the blue paint and blot any excess on kitchen paper. Stamp the crab evenly on to the mugs.

2 Allow the paint to dry. Stick the masking tape around the bottom edge of the mug. Draw the border freehand on the tape with black felt-tipped pen. Carefully cut away the bottom edge of the masking tape using a craft knife.

3 Use the cosmetic sponge to decorate the border. Use both the blue and green paints, to add depth. Sponge the handles and stamp more mugs with related motifs. Peel off the masking tape. Set the paints.

A set of delicately frosted plates would look terrific for winter dinner settings and this snowflake design is child's play to achieve. Make up as many differently designed snowflakes as you like.

Sponged Snowflake Plate

You will need

plain china plate

cleaning fluid

cloth

pencil

cup

masking film (frisket paper)

scissors

craft knife

self-healing cutting mat

sponge

paint dish

water-based ceramic paints: ice blue, dark blue and gold

1 Clean the plate. Draw round an upturned cup on to the backing paper of masking film (frisket paper) to make eight circles. Cut out the circles with scissors. Fold each circle in half. Crease each semi-circle twice to make three equal sections. Fold these sections over each other to make a triangle with a curved edge.

2 Draw a partial snowflake design on to one triangle and shade the areas that will be cut away. Ensure that parts of the folded edges remain intact. Cut out the design using a craft knife and self-healing cutting mat. Repeat to make seven more snowflake shapes. Unfold them, peel away the backing paper and position them on the plate.

3 Load a sponge cube with ice blue paint and dab it all over the plate. When dry, sponge darker blue around the outer and inner rims. Allow to dry, then dab a sponge loaded with gold paint around the edge of the plate, the inner rim and dark areas to highlight them. Remove the film snowflakes and then set the paint following the manufacturer's instructions.

Jazz up herb and spice containers to match your kitchen decor. Each of these lovely china jars bears a coloured panel which can be used to display the name of the herb contained within.

Kitchen Herb Jars

You will need

tracing paper

soft pencil

carbon paper

masking tape

6 plain china herb jars

cleaning fluid

cloth

blue chinagraph pencil

water-based enamel paints: blue, lime green, dark green and turquoise

paint palette

artist's paintbrush

dried-out felt-tipped pen

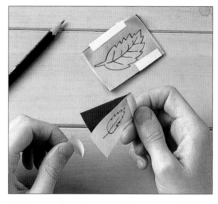

1 Draw one large and one small leaf design, each on a separate piece of tracing paper. Attach the tracing paper to carbon paper, carbon side down, with masking tape.

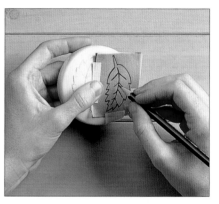

2 Clean the jars. Attach the tracing of the larger leaf on to the lid of a jar, to one side, and trace the outline with a pencil to transfer the design. Replace the tracing in another position on the lid and repeat.

3 Attach the smaller tracing to the side of a jar and trace the leaf outline on to the jar. Repeat the process to transfer the outline several times in different places around the jar, leaving a large space in the centre of one side for the "lozenge".

4 Using a blue chinagraph pencil, draw a freehand oval shape in the large space you have left. Fill in the oval with blue paint.

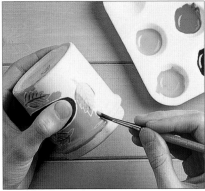

5 Before the paint dries, draw a design, pattern or a word on the oval shape, using an old dried-out felt-tipped pen. The felt tip will remove the blue paint to reveal the white china beneath.

6 Paint the herb leaves lime green. Allow the paint to dry completely. Add detail to the leaves in a darker green paint. Allow to dry.

7 Fill in the background in turquoise, leaving a thin white outline around each image. Paint the background of the lid in the same way. Leave the paint to dry. Paint the remaining jars in complementary colours.

The colour scheme of this decorative wall plate is inspired by the rich colours of medieval tapestries. Solvent-based paints are used as they are available in metallic colours which can be diluted.

Heraldic Wall Plate

You will need

large, shallow, white-glazed plate

self-sticking dots

scissors

medium and fine artist's paintbrushes

solvent-based ceramic paint: yellow, red, gold, black and green

turpentine or clear rubbing alcohol

craft knife

hard pencil

tracing paper

pair of compasses (compass)

carbon paper

masking tape

polyurethane varnish or glaze

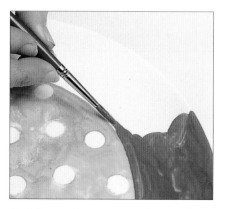

1 Stick small, sticky-backed dots at random over the middle of the plate. Cut some more of the dots in half, and stick them around the natural edge of the centre, where it meets the rim section of the plate. Press them down firmly.

2 Paint a small area of the centre with a thick coat of yellow solvent-based ceramic paint. Dip the paintbrush in turpentine or rubbing alcohol and spread the paint for a colourwashed effect. Work outwards to the edge of the centre section. Leave to dry.

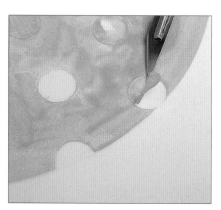

3 Carefully remove the sticky-backed dots using the edge of a craft knife. If any of the yellow paint has bled under the dots, use a fine paintbrush dipped in solvent to remove it, so that you are left with a clean outline around all the white circles.

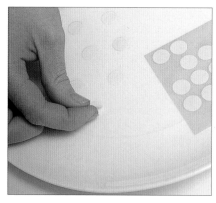

4 Using the same colourwashing technique, paint the rim of the plate red. Paint up to the yellow; do not worry if you go slightly over it. Leave the red paint to dry. Draw around the rim of the plate on to tracing paper. Measure and draw the central circle of the plate on to the tracing paper with a pair of compasses.

5 Cut out the outer ring of tracing paper and fold into eighths. The folds mark the top of each fleur-de-lis. Cut a carbon paper ring the same size. Place it face down on the rim and fix with masking tape. Open out the tracing paper and tape on top. Mark the points on the plate. Remove the carbon and tracing paper.

6 Using the template provided, draw a fleur-de-lis, slightly smaller than the rim depth, on to tracing paper. Cut a square of carbon paper the same size. Align the motif with a mark. Securing with masking tape, slip the carbon paper underneath. Transfer to the plate. Repeat around the rim.

7 Using gold paint, paint the fleur-de-lis motifs, the centres of the white dots, and dots between the fleur-de-lis. The gold ceramic paint will be quite translucent, and you may have to paint two coats, especially over the red, to achieve a rich tone. Allow the paint to dry between coats.

8 Using a fine paintbrush and black paint, carefully work around the fleur-de-lis motifs and the white dots to create a crisp outline. Leave the paint to dry.

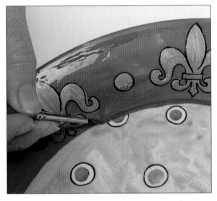

9 Using a medium paintbrush, paint a green line all around the edge of the yellow circle. Try to keep the line as even as possible. You may find it easier with a fine paintbrush, going round two or three times. Cover the paint with varnish or glaze.

Brighten up a simple and plain china lampbase with a series of fun and quirky patterns in bright colours such as turquoise, pink, lime and lilac. You will need to dismantle the base before painting it.

Patterned Lampbase

You will need
ceramic lampbase
cleaning fluid
cloth
soft pencil
tracing paper
plain paper
scissors
carbon paper
clear adhesive tape
solvent-based ceramic paints: lilac,
turquoise, pink, lime and black
medium and fine artist's paintbrushes
lampshade

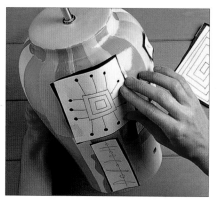

1 Clean the lampbase and remove all the electrics. Trace the background template from the back of the book on to tracing paper and transfer to a piece of paper. Using the paper as a guide, transfer the background design on to the lampbase with a soft pencil.

2 Trace the pattern templates at the back of the book on to tracing paper and transfer on to a sheet of plain paper. Cut out the designs, and attach them to carbon paper using clear adhesive tape.

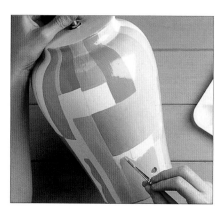

3 Paint the background of the lampbase using a medium paintbrush. First paint in the lilac sections, then add the turquoise, pink and lime. Leave the paint to dry.

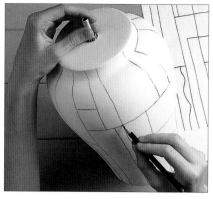

4 Arrange the designs around the painted lampbase, then fix them in place with clear adhesive tape. Use a soft pencil to transfer the design through the carbon paper on to the lampbase. Press lightly on the plain paper to leave a clear print.

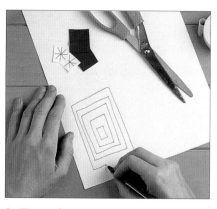

5 Using the black ceramic paint and a fine paintbrush, work carefully over the outlines made by the carbon paper. When the paint is completely dry, refit the electrics to the lampbase and attach a lampshade in a complementary colour.

Coffee cups handpainted with broad brush strokes and lots of little raised dots of paint are simpler to create than you would think...with the help of a little self-adhesive vinyl.

Leaf Motif Cup and Saucer

You will need

white ceramic cup and saucer

cleaning fluid

cloth

cotton buds (swabs)

pencil

paper

scissors

self-adhesive vinyl

green water-based ceramic paint

medium artist's paintbrush

hair dryer (optional)

craft knife

pewter acrylic paint with nozzle-tipped tube

1 Clean any grease from the china to be painted using cleaning fluid and a cloth or cotton bud (swab). Draw leaves and circles freehand on to paper. Cut them out and draw around them on the backing of the self-adhesive vinyl. Cut out. Peel away the backing paper and stick the pieces on the china.

2 Paint around the leaf and circle shapes with green water-based ceramic paint, applying several coats of paint in order to achieve a solid colour. Leave the centre circle of the saucer white. Leave each coat to air-dry before applying the next, or use a hair dryer for speed.

3 To ensure that the design has a tidy edge, cut around each sticky shape carefully with a craft knife, then peel off the sticky-backed plastic.

4 Clean up any smudges with a cotton bud dipped in acetone or water. Paint fine green lines out from the centre of each circle.

5 Using pewter paint and the nozzle-tipped paint tube, mark the outlines and details of the leaves with rows of small dots. Leave for 36 hours, then bake, following the manufacturer's instructions. The paint will withstand everyday use, but not the dishwasher.

Sunflowers seem to be perennially popular as decorating motifs. They certainly make a wonderfully cheerful design. Be adventurous and try your hand at this freehand decoration.

Sunflower Vase

You will need

plain white ceramic vase

cleaning fluid

cloth

tracing paper

soft pencil

masking tape

chinagraph pencils: yellow and blue

water-based enamel paints: yellow, pale green, light brown, dark green, very pale brown and sky blue

paint palette

medium and fine artist's paintbrushes

1 Clean the vase thoroughly. Draw a freehand sunflower on to the tracing paper and enlarge it if necessary. Fix the tracing to the vase using masking tape, and rub with a soft pencil to transfer the image.

2 Reposition the tracing paper to transfer the sunflower design all around the vase. Highlight the outline of each design with a yellow chinagraph pencil.

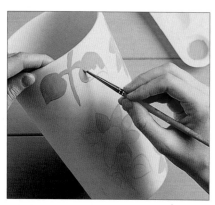

3 Fill in the petals with yellow paint and the stalks and leaves with pale green. Allow to dry. Paint the flower-head centres light brown. Include a circle of short lines around the edge of each flower centre. Allow to dry.

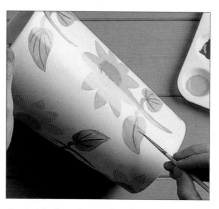

4 Add detail to the leaves using a darker shade of green. Add dabs of very pale brown to the centre of each flowerhead. Allow to dry. Fill in the background with sky blue paint, leaving a white edge showing around the flower. Allow to dry.

5 Finally, draw around the outline and central detail of each flower with a blue chinagraph pencil.

Imaginative seaside designs applied to a plain ceramic soap dish and toothbrush holder will transform the look of your bathroom, giving it a bright and cheerful underwater theme.

Seashore Bathroom Set

You will need

plain china soap dish and toothbrush holder or mug

cleaning fluid

cloth

tracing paper

soft and hard pencils

plain paper

adhesive spray

carbon paper

scissors or craft knife

masking tape

medium and fine artist's paintbrushes

water-based ceramic paints: mid-blue, ivory, turquoise, lemon, pink, white and dark blue

paint palette

1 Clean the china well. Trace the templates at the back of the book, enlarging if necessary. Transfer the designs on to plain paper. Spray the back of the paper with adhesive and stick to the back of a sheet of carbon paper. Cut out the designs, leaving a margin all round. Tape on to the china; transfer the lines with a hard pencil. Remove the carbon.

2 Using a medium paintbrush, paint a border around the soap dish, and then paint the background in mid-blue. When it is dry, paint the fish and shells, using the ivory, turquoise, lemon and pink paints. Paint the toothbrush holder in the same way.

3 When the paint is completely dry, add the final touches to the soap dish and toothbrush holder. Paint on white dots and fine squiggles to create the effect of water. Using a fine paintbrush and the dark blue paint, carefully sketch in any detailing on the fish and shells. Allow to dry.

This cheerful sun design would be particularly welcome on the breakfast table for milk, orange juice or a simple posy of flowers. The colours could be adapted to suit your other china.

Morning Sun Face

You will need

white ceramic jug (pitcher)
cleaning fluid
cloth
tracing paper
hard and soft pencils
scissors
masking tape
acrylic china paints: black, bright yellow, ochre, blue, red and white
paint palette
fine artist's paintbrushes
hair dryer (optional)

1 Clean the china to remove any grease. Trace the template at the back of the book, try it for size and enlarge it if necessary. Cut it out roughly then rub over the back with a soft pencil. Make several cuts around the edge of the circle, so that the template will lie flat, and tape it in place. Draw over the outlines with a hard pencil to transfer the design.

2 Go over the sun's outlines with black paint and allow to dry; a hair dryer can speed up the process. Paint the main face and inner rays in bright yellow and then paint the cheeks and other parts of the rays in ochre.

3 Paint the background blue, then add fine details to the sun's face. Highlight each eye with a white dot. Set, following the manufacturer's instructions. The paint will withstand everyday use, but not the dishwasher.

The application of a few blocks of gold colour, highlighted by sketched leaf outlines which are positioned like falling leaves, quickly turns a plain white coffee pot into an elegant piece of ceramic ware.

Autumn Leaf Coffee Pot

You will need

hard and soft pencils
stencil cardboard
craft knife
metal ruler
self-healing cutting mat
carbon paper
fine felt-tipped pen
plain ceramic coffee pot
cleaning fluid
cloth
masking tape
sponge
water-based ceramic paints:
gold and black
paint dish
fine artist's paintbrush

1 Use a pencil to draw an irregular four-sided shape, approximately 2cm/¾in square, on to a piece of stencil cardboard. Using a sharp craft knife, a metal ruler and self-healing cutting mat, cut the shape away, leaving the cardboard border intact.

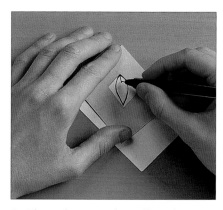

2 Place the stencil cardboard over a piece of carbon paper, carbon side down. Gently draw the outline of a leaf with a centre vein through the stencil hole on to the piece of carbon paper, using a fine felt-tipped pen.

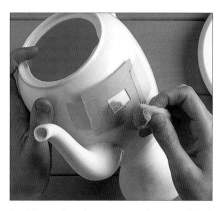

3 Clean the china using cleaning fluid and a cloth. Attach the stencil to the pot with masking tape. Load a small sponge cube with gold paint. Lightly dab it over the stencil, without going over the outside edge of the cardboard. Leave to dry. Remove the stencil.

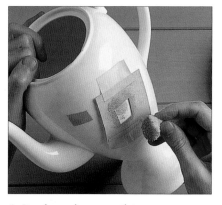

4 Replace the stencil in a new position on the coffee pot, rotating it slightly. Avoid sticking the masking tape over the previously painted shape. Dab the stencil with gold paint as before. Repeat the process to create a random pattern over the entire coffee pot, including the spout and lid.

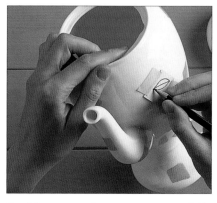

5 Using masking tape, carefully attach the carbon paper with the leaf drawing over a stencilled gold shape so that the leaf outline overlaps the edge of colour. With a sharp soft pencil, lightly transfer the leaf shape on to the coffee pot.

6 Remove the carbon paper and trace the shape over the remaining blocks of gold colour. Position the leaves at slightly different angles each time.

7 Darken the leaf outlines with black paint, using a fine paintbrush. Leave to dry. Fill in the leaf veins with black paint. Leave to dry.

8 Finish off the design by painting the knob of the coffee pot lid with gold paint. Allow to dry.

Stylized holly leaves and berries decorate the rim of this festive oval platter, while the gold outlines and gold-spattered centre add seasonal glamour. Display this painted plate heaped high with mince pies.

Holly Christmas Platter

You will need

masking film (frisket paper)
white glazed oval plate
scissors
craft knife
hard and soft pencils
watercolour paper or
flexible cardboard
fine felt-tipped pen (optional)
medium and fine artist's paintbrushes
solvent-based ceramic paints: rich dark
green, bright red, maroon, gold
white spirit (paint thinner)
toothbrush
paint palette
polyurethane varnish

1 Cut out a rectangle of masking film (frisket paper), roughly the size of the plate. Take the backing off and stick on to the plate, pressing it outwards from the centre. Using a craft knife, cut around the inner oval edge of the rim to mask out the plate centre. Remove the excess.

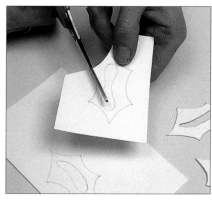

2 Using the template provided, draw two or three holly leaves with an elongated oval for the midrib on to watercolour paper or flexible cardboard. Give the leaves different curving shapes to add interest. Cut out the leaves and centres using a craft knife or small sharp scissors.

3 Arrange the leaves around the rim, leaving room for stems and a line at the top and bottom of the rim. Mark with a pencil where the first leaf starts. Fill in any space with extra berries. Draw around the leaves using a fine felt-tipped pen or pencil.

4 Add the stems, some straight, others curved, some single, others joining to form sprigs. To fill the gaps, draw berries singly or in pairs.

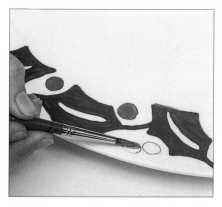

5 Using a medium paintbrush, paint the holly leaves and stems green, leaving the midrib white. Allow to dry, then add touches of green to highlight. Allow to dry, then paint the berries red and leave to dry.

6 Paint the maroon background. Use a fine paintbrush to go round the leaves, stems and berries first, leaving a narrow white outline, as shown. Infill the awkward background spaces with a fine paintbrush, then switch to a medium paintbrush for the rest. Allow to dry.

7 Using a medium paintbrush, paint a gold outline around the leaves and berries, and along one side of the stems. Try to leave as much white outline as possible exposed. Leave to dry. Using the edge of a craft knife, lift the masking paper off the middle of the plate.

8 To spatter the platter gold, mix two parts paint to one part white spirit (paint thinner). Pour a little paint into a saucer, and then spatter the platter with gold by rubbing your thumb over a toothbrush dipped in paint. Leave to dry. Paint a narrow red band around the rim. When dry, coat with varnish.

Imagine the delight this painted tea set featuring playful rabbits will bring to a child you know. This fun design is easy to accomplish using the templates provided; they can be enlarged as necessary.

Fun Bunnies Tea Set

You will need

plain china mug, plate and bowl

cleaning fluid

cloth

tracing paper

soft pencil

plain paper

adhesive spray

carbon paper

scissors

clear adhesive tape

felt-tipped pen

cotton bud (swab)

water-based enamel paints: yellow, turquoise, red, green and blue

paint palette

medium and fine artist's paintbrushes

1 Thoroughly clean the china mug, plate and bowl with cleaning fluid and a cloth. Trace the templates for the rabbits and flower at the back of the book and transfer them to a piece of plain paper. Spray the back of the paper with glue and place it on top of a sheet of carbon paper, carbon side down. Cut out around the drawings, leaving a narrow margin.

2 Arrange the cut-out drawings around the china mug, plate and bowl, securing them in place with clear adhesive tape. Go over the designs with a felt-tipped pen to transfer the designs to the china pieces. Remove the cut-outs and clean any smudges carefully with a cotton bud (swab).

3 Paint the background areas of the centre of the bowl in yellow.

4 Paint the remaining background areas, around the rim of the bowl, in turquoise. Leave to dry.

5 Begin to paint in the details. Here the flowers are painted red, turquoise and green.

◀ **6** Using a fine paintbrush, paint over the outlines of the large rabbits and flowers with blue paint. Paint over the outlines of the smaller rabbits on the rim of the plate with blue paint.

▶ **7** Paint the mug handle turquoise. Allow to dry. The pieces should be fired in a kiln to make them foodsafe.

Kitchen storage jars are always useful, and when adorned with unique bold designs such as these colourful vegetable shapes they add a quirky and bright visual detail to your kitchen.

Vegetable Storage Jars

You will need

tracing paper

soft pencil

plain paper

adhesive spray

carbon paper

scissors

plain china storage jars

cleaning fluid

cloth

clear adhesive tape

felt-tipped pen

medium and fine artist's paintbrushes

water-based enamel paints: turquoise, coral, ivory, blue and yellow

paint palette

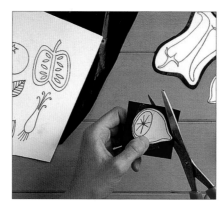

1 Trace the templates at the back of the book and enlarge if necessary. Transfer the designs on to a piece of plain paper. Spray the back of the paper with glue and stick it on to a sheet of carbon paper, carbon side down. Cut out the designs leaving a margin all round.

2 Clean the china storage jars, using cleaning fluid and a cloth. Tape some of the designs on to one of the jars. Go over the outlines lightly with a felt-tipped pen to transfer the designs to the jar. Remove the carbon paper designs and repeat the process for the other jars.

3 Using a medium paintbrush, paint in the turquoise background colour between the vegetable designs on the sides of the storage jars and their lids. Allow the paint to dry completely before proceeding to the next stage – this may take several days.

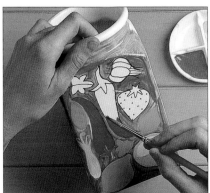

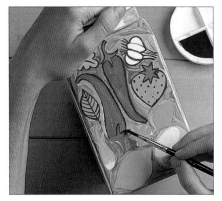

4 Mix up some red paint from the coral and ivory and paint the chillies. Mix the blue and yellow paint and paint the green of the vegetable leaves. Allow to dry.

5 Using a fine paintbrush and the blue paint, sketch in the detailing for the vegetables.

6 Paint the jar rims with the yellow paint and add some small ivory dots in the turquoise background area for decoration. Allow the paint to dry completely before using the jars.

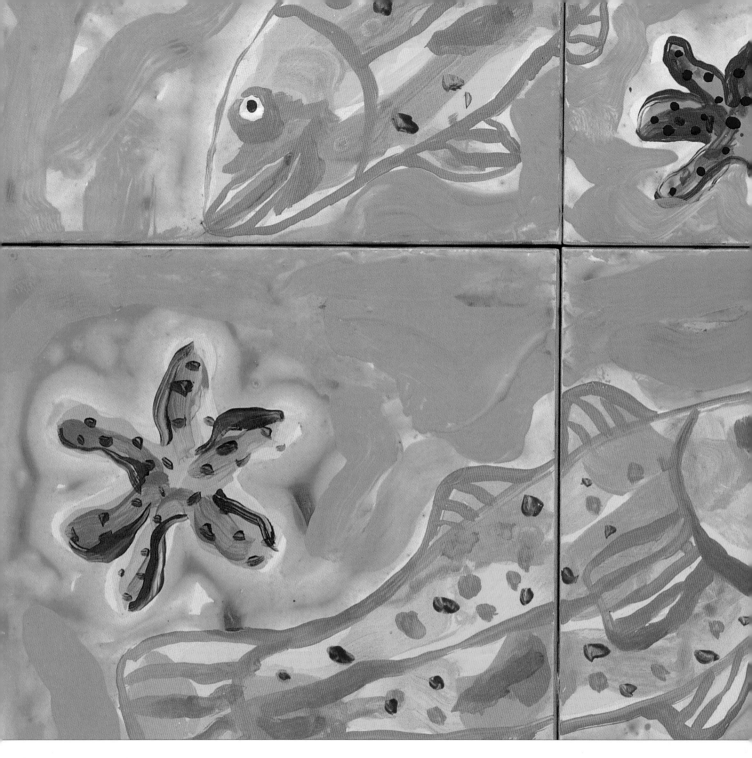

Decorating Tiles

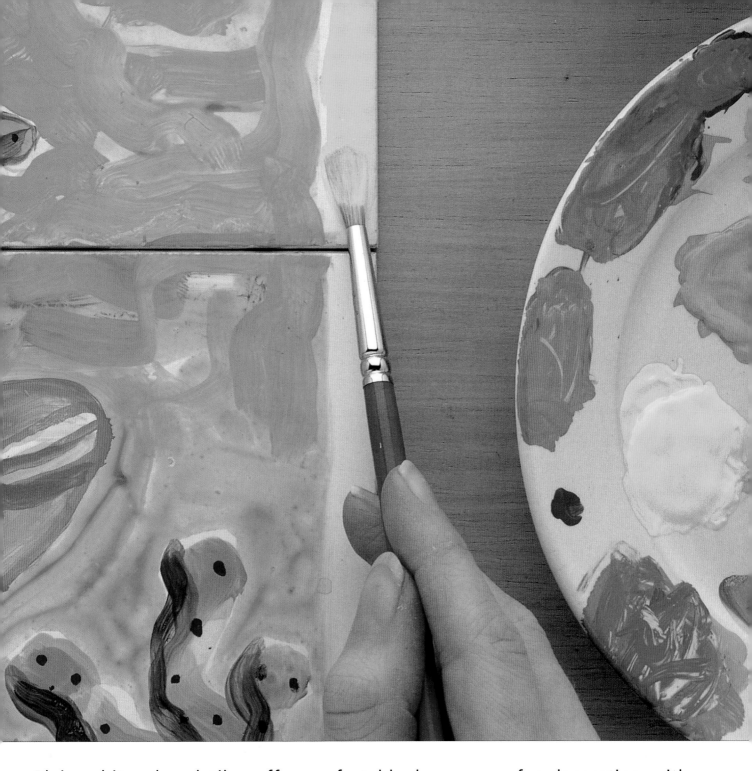

Plain white glazed tiles offer perfect blank canvases for decorating with paint, and their flat surface makes it so easy to do. Use single tiles for pot or pan stands, or plan a small-scale panel design over four or six tiles to add decorative details to plain walls, floors and splashbacks. Like ceramics, tiles can be decorated in a myriad of ways, using different techniques and finishes depending upon their intended use.

White, glazed tiles are inexpensive, making this craft truly accessible to everyone. Painted tiles can add instant cheer to a room and help to complement existing features and fittings.

Materials

domestic oven are available. Make sure your tiles are sturdy enough to be heated in this way.

Masking tape

This removable paper tape is available in different widths. It is used to mask off areas to be painted, and also to hold stencils and tracings in place.

PVA (white) glue

Use this to attach decoupage images.

Ready-mixed and powdered grout and colourant

Powdered grout is more economical than ready-mixed grout. Mix with water to a creamy paste, following the manufacturer's instructions. Powdered grout comes in different colours, or can also be coloured with grout colourant. Wear a protective face mask, safety goggles and rubber (latex) gloves when handling or mixing powdered materials.

Stencil cardboard

This manila cardboard has been impregnated with oil and is available in several thicknesses. It is durable and water-resistant and it makes strong stencils with crisp edges that last well. The cardboard is easy to cut with a craft knife and cutting mat.

Tile adhesive

Use this to glue tiles to the wall.

Ceramic wall tiles

Glazed wall tiles are waterproof and hardwearing, though brittle. They are thinner than floor tiles, usually about 5mm/¼in thick, and come in a huge range of colours, designs, finishes and sizes. The tiles used the most in this chapter are plain white tiles as they allow plenty of scope for decoration.

Cold-set ceramic paints

Ceramic paints that are non-toxic, water-based and cold-set are the choice recommended for painting tiles. They are available in a wide range of colours and can be mixed or thinned with water. The paints set to a very durable finish after 48–72 hours drying time, but they are not as durable as unpainted glazed tiles. Care must be taken when grouting – keep the grout to the edges of the tile only. Do not clean the tiles vigorously but wipe them with a damp cloth. If more permanent decoration is required, heat-fixable paints that are set in a

You will not need to purchase many items of equipment for painting ceramic tiles, but try to ensure you buy good quality paintbrushes as they will give a much more professional finish to your craftwork.

Equipment

Craft knife
This tool is very useful for making clean, precise cuts. Always cut away from your body and use a metal ruler to cut against.

Lint-free cloth
Use for polishing tiles after grouting.

Metal ruler
This is very useful for marking out guidelines for cutting stencils or for other decoration.

Notched spreader
Use to spread tile adhesive on tiles.

Paint-mixing container
Make sure you have enough mixed paint for the work, as it is impossible to match colours later.

Safety goggles
These should always be worn when handling powdered materials, such as grout or grout colourant, as well as for cutting tiles.

Self-healing cutting mat
Use this mat to protect your work surface when cutting anything with a craft knife.

Set square
Use to align guide battens and to check that each row of tiles is straight.

Spirit (carpenter's) level
This will ensure a straight line when you are fixing a guide batten.

Sponge
Use a damp sponge to remove excess tile adhesive and grout from tiles.

Tile spacers
These are small plastic crosses that are placed between tiles to create regular gaps for grouting. They are useful if you are using tiles without in-built spacer lugs. Some spacers are removed before grouting after the adhesive has dried. Others are much thinner and can simply be grouted over.

Tracing paper
Use to trace motifs from the back of the book and transfer to plain tiles.

You will also find the following items useful: face mask, hammer, hand-held tile cutter, leather gloves, paintbrushes, pencils, rubber (latex) gloves, tile-cutting machine, tile file.

Tiling a wall with your completed painted tiles can be challenging depending on the size of area you are tiling and the number of tiles that have to be cut. The following tips will help the beginner.

Techniques

Cutting tiles

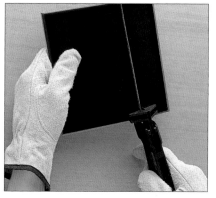

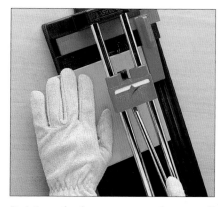

1 To use a hand-held tile cutter, first measure the width required and deduct 2mm/1⁄16in to allow for grout. Mark the cutting line on the tile. Place the cutting wheel against a short metal ruler and score the line once only to pierce the glaze.

2 Wearing protective leather gloves and safety goggles, place the tile as far as it will go into the jaws of the cutter with the scored line positioned in the centre, then close the handles of the cutter to snap the tile in two.

3 Manual tile-cutting machines will cut tiles up to about 5mm/1⁄4in thick quickly and accurately, and they have a useful measuring gauge. Adjust the gauge to the correct width, then pull the wheel once down the tile to score a cutting line. Snap along this line.

4 Wearing protective leather gloves, a face mask and safety goggles, use a tile file to smooth along the cut edge of the tile if desired.

Right: Tile cutters, grout, tiles and a straightedge are just a few of the items you will need to tile an area.

Mixing grout

When colouring grout, mix enough for the whole project, as it is difficult to match the colour in a second batch.

1 When mixing up powdered grout, add the powder to a measured amount of water, rather than the other way round, otherwise the mixture may be lumpy. Mix the powder thoroughly into the water. Always wear rubber (latex) gloves, a protective face mask and goggles.

2 Grout colourant can be added to the powdered grout before mixing it with water. Wear protective clothing as for powdered grout, and then mix with water in the proportion advised by the manufacturer.

Removing grease

You may wish to decorate tiles that are not in pristine condition. It is essential to start with a clean surface to ensure an even application of paint. To remove grease and fingerprints from the surface of tiles before you paint them, wipe with a solution of 1 part malt vinegar to 10 of water.

Below: Single painted tiles can be used to break up a plainly tiled wall.

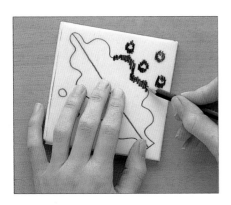

Transferring a design

Cut a piece of tracing paper the same size as the tile. Centre the design, then trace it. Centre the paper design-side down on the tile, matching the edges. Scribble over the lines to transfer to the tile. If the design is not symmetrical, scribble over the lines on to a piece of paper. Place the tracing design-side up on the tile and redraw over the original lines.

Tiling a Wall

It is vital to prepare the surface to be tiled properly so that the tiles will adhere well. And, as with most techniques, the more you practise, the more skilled you will become.

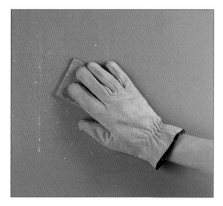

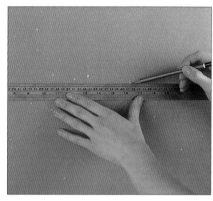

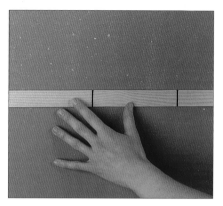

1 To prepare wall surfaces, remove wallpaper or flaking paint, and fill cracks and holes. Leave new plaster to dry for 4 weeks and seal it before tiling. Wash emulsion (latex) paint with sugar soap then sand, wearing a protective face mask, to provide a key (scuffed surface) for the tiles.

2 It is important to calculate the number of tiles before you begin. Using a long metal ruler or metal tape measure, first find the centre of the wall. You usually need to cut some tiles to fit the wall. Set the cut tiles in the corners or at the edges of walls, where they will be least noticeable.

3 Mark a wooden strip with divisions one tile wide plus an extra 2mm/¹⁄₁₆in for grouting either side. Place in the centre of the wall, holding it first vertically, then horizontally. If the edges of the wall fall between two divisions on the strip, you can see the width of the cut tiles needed.

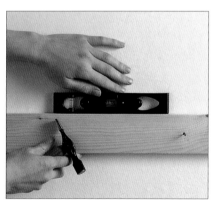

4 Wall tiles are applied upwards from a baseline, usually one tile up from a skirting (base) board, sink or the side of a bath. Draw the baseline, then attach a batten with the top edge along the line. Hammer the nails in part-way, then check with a spirit (carpenter's) level that it is straight.

5 Use a plumbline to establish a true vertical at the side of the batten. Using a set square, draw a second line at this point to mark the side edge of the first complete tile in each row. Attach a batten along the outside of the line, hammering it in place with nails as before.

6 Wearing rubber (latex) gloves, spread a thin layer of tile adhesive (approximately 3mm/¹⁄₈in deep) over the wall, inside the battens. Work on a small area at a time, otherwise the adhesive will dry before you have time to tile the wall.

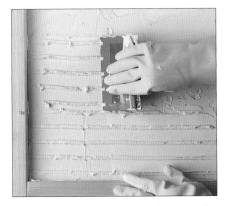

7 Using a notched spreader, "comb" the tile adhesive to provide a key (scuff) to the surface so that the tiles will adhere well. If you do not provide a good surface, the finished result will be less successful.

8 Starting in the bottom corner, position the first tile in place, where the two wooden battens meet. Push it into position with a slight twisting movement of the wrist, to ensure that the back of the tile is completely coated with tile adhesive.

9 Some tiles have built-in spacer lugs. If not, use plastic spacers at the corners of the tiles so that the grouting lines are regular. Remove excess adhesive with a damp sponge before it hardens. As you go, check the tiles with a spirit (carpenter's) level every few rows to make sure they are straight, and adjust as necessary.

10 When the tile adhesive is dry, remove the battens. Add cut tiles at the edges of the tiled areas if necessary. Leave for about 24 hours. Using the rubber edge of the spreader, apply grout to the gaps between the tiles. It is important to use the right type of grout depending on where the tiles are used. Make sure that the gaps are completely filled, or small holes will appear as the grout dries.

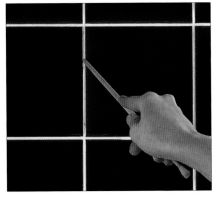

11 When the grout has hardened slightly, pull a round-ended stick along the gaps between the tiles to give a smooth finish to the grout. Add a little more grout at this stage if you notice any small holes in the previous layer.

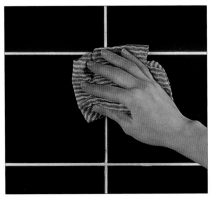

12 Leave the grout to set for about 30 minutes, then remove the excess with a damp sponge. When the grout is completely dry, polish the surface of the tiles with a dry, lint-free cloth to remove any remaining smudges and to give a glossy finish.

These cheerful tiles are based on simple Mexican designs. The motifs are easy to do so you can paint a set quite quickly. They will add a colourful touch to a kitchen wall, as an all-over design or a border.

Mexican Folk Art Tiles

You will need
soft pencil
clean, off-white glazed ceramic tiles
medium and fine paintbrushes
non-toxic, water-based, cold-set
ceramic paints
paint palette

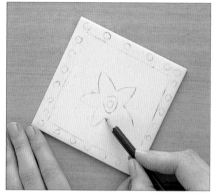

1 Using a soft pencil, draw a simple flower and spotted border design on one of the tiles.

2 Fill in the petals, using a medium paintbrush. Add a dot of contrasting paint for the flower centre.

3 Paint the border in a dark colour, leaving the spots blank. Using a fine paintbrush and various colours, paint a small spot in the centre of each blank spot. Leave to dry.

Children will love these chunky letter tiles. Use them to make a panel or a frieze around a bedroom or playroom wall, mixing the letters at random or spelling out a name. Use non-toxic ceramic paints.

Alphabet Tiles

You will need

fine black felt-tipped pen

clean, plain white glazed ceramic tiles

fine and medium artist's paintbrushes

non-toxic, water-based, cold-set

ceramic paint: black

paint palette

1 Using a fine felt-tipped pen, draw the outline of the letter on to one tile, extending the lines right to the edges of the tile. Using a fine paintbrush, go over the outlines with black paint. Leave to dry.

2 Using a medium paintbrush, paint bold black stripes down one side of the tile, as shown.

3 Leaving the letter white, fill in the rest of the design with dots, spots and fine lines. Leave to dry thoroughly.

These Roman numerals are timeless and elegant. You could paint them to make up a particular and memorable date, such as the year your house was built, an anniversary or an important birthday.

Roman Numeral Tiles

You will need

scissors

scrap paper

stencil cardboard

clean, plain white glazed ceramic tiles

metal ruler

pencil

self-healing cutting mat

craft knife

small stencil brush

non-toxic, water-based, cold-set ceramic paint: blue

spray ceramic varnish

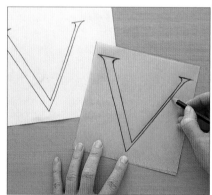

1 Cut a piece of scrap paper and a piece of stencil cardboard the same size as the tile. Using a ruler and pencil, draw the numeral on the scrap paper. Transfer the numeral on to the stencil cardboard.

2 Place the stencil cardboard on a cutting mat. Using a craft knife, carefully cut away the cardboard inside the pencil lines. Place the stencil on the tile, aligning the corners, and stipple blue paint on to the tile. Leave to dry.

3 Working in a well-ventilated area, place the painted tile on a large sheet of scrap paper. Holding the spray can about 30cm/12in from the tile, spray it all over with an even layer of the ceramic varnish.

Trace these jolly designs from the back of the book, outline the shapes in a dark colour, then fill them in with jewel-bright shades. The bold designs are ideal for a child's bathroom.

Cartoon Tiles

You will need

tracing paper

pencil

clean, plain white glazed ceramic tiles

fine artist's paintbrush

non-toxic, water-based, cold-set ceramic paints in various colours

paint palette

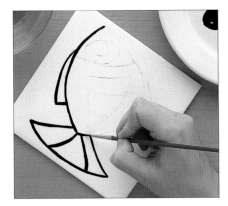

1 Trace the motifs provided and transfer to the tile. Using dark green, paint over the outlines. Add spots to the background area. Leave to dry.

2 Colour in the design. Paint spots on the fish. Leave to dry thoroughly.

The details on these tiles are incised into the wet paint in a traditional form of decoration known as sgraffito. Paint a set of tiles one at a time so that the paint does not dry before you add the sgraffito.

Sgraffito Fish Tiles

You will need

chinagraph pencil (optional)

clean, plain white glazed ceramic tiles

tracing paper (optional)

pencil (optional)

non-toxic, water-based, cold-set ceramic paints: dark blue and turquoise

medium artist's paintbrushes

paint palette

engraver's scribing tool or sharp pencil

varnish as recommended by the paint manufacturer

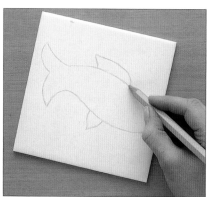

1 Using a chinagraph pencil, draw the outline of the fish on to the tile. Alternatively, enlarge the template from the back of the book and transfer to the tile.

2 Fill in the fish shape with dark blue paint using a medium paintbrush. While the paint is still wet, scratch decorative details on to the fish shape with an engraver's scribing tool or sharp pencil.

3 Fill in the background with turquoise paint, leaving a fine white outline around the fish. Scratch a swirl at each corner, as shown. Leave to dry, then seal the surface with a coat of the recommended varnish.

These deliciously pretty tiles are sponged in two tones of pink, then painted with tiny rosebuds. Sponging is simple and an ordinary bath sponge will suffice, provided it has a well-defined, open texture.

Rosebud Tiles

You will need

non-toxic, water-based, cold-set ceramic paints: pink, white, red and green

paint palette

natural sponge or highly textured nylon sponge

clean, plain white glazed ceramic tiles

medium artist's paintbrush

1 Mix the pink paint with white to give a very pale pink. Dip the sponge in the paint and apply randomly over the tile, leaving white spaces here and there. Leave to dry.

2 Add more pink to the mixed paint to darken it. Sponge this colour over the tile, allowing the first colour to show through. Leave to dry, then sponge a little white paint on top.

3 Using red paint and a paintbrush, paint rosebud shapes randomly on to the sponged tile. Using green paint, add three leaves to each rosebud as shown. Leave to dry thoroughly.

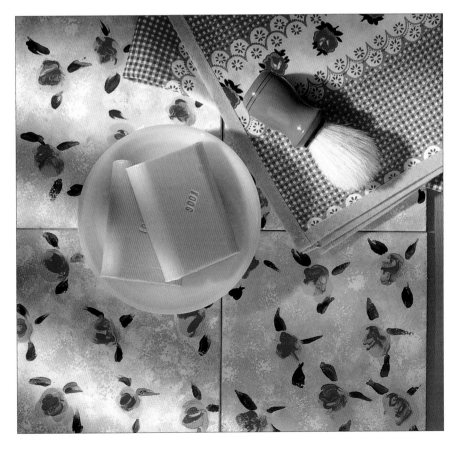

Four plain ceramic tiles combine here to make an attractive and striking wall mural, reminiscent of Japanese art in its graphic simplicity and clear, calm blue-and-white colour scheme.

Maritime Tile Mural

You will need

soft and hard pencils

tracing paper

masking tape

4 clean, plain white glazed 15cm/6in square ceramic tiles

chinagraph pencil

non-toxic, water-based, cold-set ceramic paints: mid-blue, dark blue and black

paint palette

small and fine artist's paintbrushes

1 Trace the template from the back of the book and enlarge, if necessary. Tape the tracing to the four tiles, positioning it centrally. Transfer the outline to the tiles with a hard pencil.

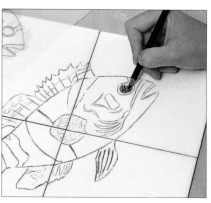

2 Trace over the outline again with a chinagraph pencil. Draw the border freehand, and add any extra details to the fish. Follow the finished picture as a guide.

3 Keep the tiles together as you paint. Using the ceramic paints, fill in the fish shape. First, paint the main part of the fish mid-blue.

4 Paint the detail and the border dark blue. Highlight the scales with black. Set the paint following the manufacturer's instructions. The painted tiles will withstand gentle cleaning.

This quirky cherub tile panel will add cheery individuality to any wall. Decorated in the style of Majolica ware, with bright colours and a stylized design, this romantic cherub is easy to paint.

Cherub Tiles

You will need
pencil
tracing paper
4 clean, plain white, glazed, square
ceramic tiles
fine artist's paintbrushes
non-toxic, water-based, cold-set
ceramic paints: dark blue,
yellow and red
paint palette

1 Trace the template from the back of the book. Enlarge the design on to a piece of tracing paper. Use a pencil to transfer a quarter of the design to each ceramic tile.

2 With a fine brush, and dark blue paint, paint over the main outline on each tile. If required, heat the tiles in the oven for the time specified by the paint manufacturer, to set the outline.

3 Fill in the wings, hair and drapery with yellow paint. Allow the paint to dry. Mix yellow with red to add darker tones, using the finished picture as a guide. Bake the tiles again, to prevent the colours from smudging.

4 With diluted blue paint, mark in the shadows on the cherub's face and body. Go over any areas that need to be defined with more blue paint. Paint the corner motifs freehand and then bake for the final time.

This is a great idea for decorating plain ceramic tiles, which could then be framed and hung on the wall. Alternatively, you could break up a plain white tiled surface with random floral tiles.

Floral Tiles

You will need
tracing paper
soft and hard pencils
masking tape
clean, plain white glazed ceramic tiles
medium and fine artist's paintbrushes
non-toxic, water-based, cold-set
ceramic paints: green, yellow,
red and blue
paint palette and jar

1 Trace the template at the back of the book and enlarge it. Turn the paper over and rub over the outline with a pencil. Tape the transfer to the tile and draw over the outline with a hard pencil to transfer the motif on to the tile.

2 Using a medium paintbrush and thin layers of paint, colour in the leaves and petals. If required, bake in the oven to set the paint, according to the paint manufacturer's instructions.

3 With a fine paintbrush and blue paint, draw in the outline and detail of the petals, leaves and stalk. Paint dots in the centre of the flower. Transfer the corner motifs, and paint them blue with a fine paintbrush. Set the paint by baking the tile. The tile will withstand gentle cleaning.

These Florentine-style tiles are based on ceramic decoration of the Renaissance. A single tile could be a focal point in a bathroom, or you could arrange several together to form interesting repeat patterns.

Italianate Tiles

You will need

clean, plain white glazed square tiles

tracing paper

soft and hard pencils

masking tape

non-toxic, water-based, cold-set ceramic paints: mid-green, dark blue-green, rust-red and dark blue

medium and fine artist's paintbrushes

paint palette

2 Paint the leaf in mid-green paint and allow to dry. You may need to mix colours to achieve the shades you require. Using a dark blue-green, paint over the outline and mark in the leaf veins. Paint a dot in each corner of the tile in the same colour.

3 Paint a border of rust-coloured leaves and a slightly larger leaf in each corner. Paint a curved scroll at both sides of the large leaf in dark blue. When the paint is completely dry, if required, set it in the oven according to the manufacturer's instructions.

1 Wash and dry the tiles thoroughly. Enlarge the template at the back of the book to fit the size of your tiles. Trace the main motif (and also the border if you wish) and rub the back of the tracing with a soft pencil. Position the tracing on each tile, secure with tape, and draw over the outline with a hard pencil.

This design of a delightful vase of flowers is based on a tile design from the Urbino area of northern Italy, where the Majolica style of pottery decoration developed in the 15th century.

Majolica Tile

You will need

tracing paper

pencil

clean, plain white glazed ceramic tile

fine artist's paintbrushes

non-toxic, water-based, cold-set ceramic paints: yellow, orange, royal blue, white, light green and dark green

paint palette

water-based acrylic varnish

1 Trace the vase of flowers design from the back of the book, enlarging it if necessary, and transfer it on to the tile. Begin to paint the design with a fine paintbrush, starting with the palest tones of each colour.

2 Carefully paint in the foliage with light and dark green paint, leaving each colour to dry before applying the next. Add white to orange paint to create a paler shade. Use this to paint the top and bottom of the vase. Using darker orange, fill in the flower centres and emphasize the shape of the vase.

3 Using royal blue paint, outline the shapes of the flowers and vase. Add the vase handles and decorative details to the flowerheads. Leave the tile to dry, then seal the surface with two coats of acrylic varnish, allowing the first coat to dry before applying the second, if required.

Translucent ceramic paints give this exotic tile the rich, glowing colours associated with Byzantine art. The decorative bird motif is taken from a cloisonné enamel panel originally decorated with precious stones.

Byzantine Bird Tile

You will need

tracing paper

pencil

clean, plain white glazed ceramic tile

non-toxic, water-based, cold-set ceramic paints in a variety of rich colours

fine artist's paintbrushes

paint palette

gold felt-tipped pen

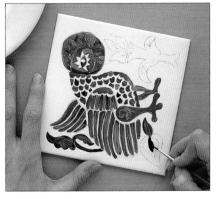

1 Trace the bird design from the back of the book, enlarging it if necessary, and transfer on to the tile. Paint the bird's head and legs, then start to paint the features, using bright colours.

2 Paint the plants, using your choice of colours. Leave to dry completely.

3 Using a gold felt-tipped pen, draw an outline around every part of the design. As a final touch, add decorative gold details to the bird's feathers and the plants.

The tile-making centre of Puebla in Mexico has been famous for its vibrant, colourful designs since the 17th century. These tiles take their inspiration from the colourful patterns of the Mexican style.

Pueblan Tiles

You will need

pencil

metal ruler

clean, plain white glazed ceramic tiles

non-toxic, water-based, cold-set ceramic paints:

orange, yellow, royal blue and turquoise

paint palette

medium artist's paintbrushes

1 Using a pencil and ruler, lightly draw a narrow border around the edge of the tile. Draw a square in all four corners. Paint the borders orange and the squares yellow.

2 Using the same colours, paint a design in the centre of the tile, as shown. Leave to dry completely.

3 Outline the borders and squares in royal blue paint. Then, starting just inside the border at each corner, paint a series of blue arcs, as shown.

4 To decorate the central motif, paint blue circle and diamond shapes over the orange and yellow design, as shown. Add a scalloped edging around the circle and diamond.

5 Using orange paint, paint a small quarter-circle in each corner of the tile to form the repeat. Finally, fill in the background with turquoise paint. Leave to dry completely.

These elegant and highly stylized designs are inspired by the work of Scottish artist Charles Rennie Mackintosh and the Glasgow School of Art at the turn of the 20th century.

Art Nouveau Tiles

You will need

tracing paper

pencil

clean, plain white glazed ceramic tiles

scissors

stencil cardboard

craft knife

self-healing cutting mat

repositionable spray adhesive

large and fine artist's paintbrushes

non-toxic, water-based, cold-set

ceramic paints: dark green, light

green, deep red and white

paint palette

water-based acrylic varnish

1 Enlarge the designs at the back of the book to fit your tiles. Cut two pieces of stencil cardboard to the size of the tiles and transfer one design to each. Using a craft knife and a cutting mat, cut away the centre of each design. Coat the back of the stencils with adhesive. Place the stem stencil on a tile. Using a dry paintbrush, apply dark green paint to the stems and light green for the leaves.

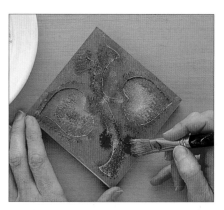

2 Allow the paint to dry completely, then use a clean, dry paintbrush to add a little deep red paint to pick out the thorns on the stem. You might also like to try reversing the stem stencil on some of the tiles, which will make the overall effect more symmetrical.

3 Mix deep red paint with white to make a dusky pink shade. Use this colour to stencil the rose motif on to another tile with a dry paintbrush. Leave the paint to dry.

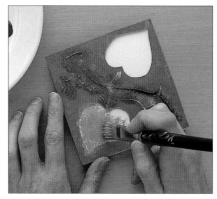

4 Add deep red around the edges of the petals to emphasize the rose shape and give it depth.

5 Using a paintbrush, add a few green dots in the centre of the rose. Leave to dry, then seal the surface of the tiles with two coats of varnish, allowing them to dry between coats, if required.

This cheerful panel is painted freehand across a block of tiles. The paint is applied in several layers, working from light to dark, to give depth and to intensify the colours.

Underwater Panel

You will need

clean, plain white glazed ceramic tiles

soft pencil

non-toxic, water-based, cold-set ceramic paints: orange, blue, green, white and red

fine and medium artist's paintbrushes

paint palette

1 Arrange the tiles as close together as possible. Use a soft pencil to sketch your design on the tiles, leaving room around the panel for the border.

2 Starting with the lightest tones of each colour, paint in the fish, shell and seaweed motifs. Allow patches of the white background to show through. Leave to dry.

3 Using medium tones of each colour, loosely paint darker areas to give depth to the sea motifs.

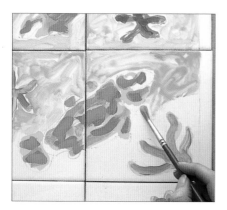

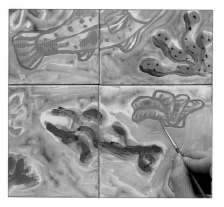

4 Fill in the background sea with diluted blue paint, allowing some of the white to show through.

5 Using a fine paintbrush and a darker tone of each colour, outline the fish, shell and seaweed motifs. Add decorative details, as shown.

6 Using a broad paintbrush, paint a border around the panel. Take the paint over the edges of the tiles where they butt up so there are no ugly gaps. Leave to dry.

This sumptuous and decadent tile is not intended for practical use but to be displayed. The surface is covered with a composite metal leaf, then decorated with a decoupage image photocopied from a book.

Silver Decoupage Tiles

You will need

plain white glazed ceramic tile

cleaning fluid

cloth

water-based Italian size and brush

aluminium composite loose leaf

large, soft brush

purple water-based ink

black and white photocopy

scissors

PVA (white) glue

ceramic tile varnish

1 Clean the tile surface thoroughly to remove any grease. Apply a thin, even coat of size, making sure that the whole surface is covered. Leave it for 15–20 minutes until the size is tacky.

2 Carefully lay the aluminium leaf on the tile. Use a large, dry, soft brush to burnish the aluminium leaf flat and remove any excess.

3 Paint a thin wash of diluted purple ink over the photocopy and leave to dry. Cut out the image. Apply a thin coat of PVA (white) glue to the back and position it on the tile, smoothing the paper down gently in order to remove any air bubbles.

4 Leave the image to dry thoroughly. Seal the surface of the tile with two thin coats of ceramic varnish, allowing the first coat to dry for about 30 minutes before applying the second.

Based on a design by William Morris from 1870, the flowing lines of the flower painting are typical of his bold style. Morris's tiles were often manufactured by designer William de Morgan.

William Morris Tiles

You will need

tracing paper

pencil

4 clean, plain white glazed ceramic tiles

scissors

ballpoint pen

non-toxic, water-based, cold-set ceramic paints: blue, dark green and white

paint palette

medium and fine artist's paintbrushes

1 Enlarge the design from the back of the book so that each square fits on to one tile. Cut it into four separate patterns. Transfer each pattern on to a tile, drawing over the lines with a ballpoint pen.

2 Dilute some of the blue paint, then fill in the two main flower shapes with a medium paintbrush. Leave the paint to dry before proceeding to the next stage.

3 Using undiluted blue paint and a fine paintbrush, work the detailing on the flower petals as shown, to add definition.

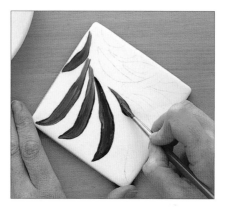

4 Using a medium paintbrush, fill in the leaves with dark green paint. The slightly streaky effect that is left by the bristles will add movement to the design. Leave the paint to dry. Highlight the leaves with white veins.

5 Paint green leaves on the flower tiles. Leave to dry, then highlight with white veins as before. Add detailing and fine outlines to the flowers. Leave the tiles to dry completely.

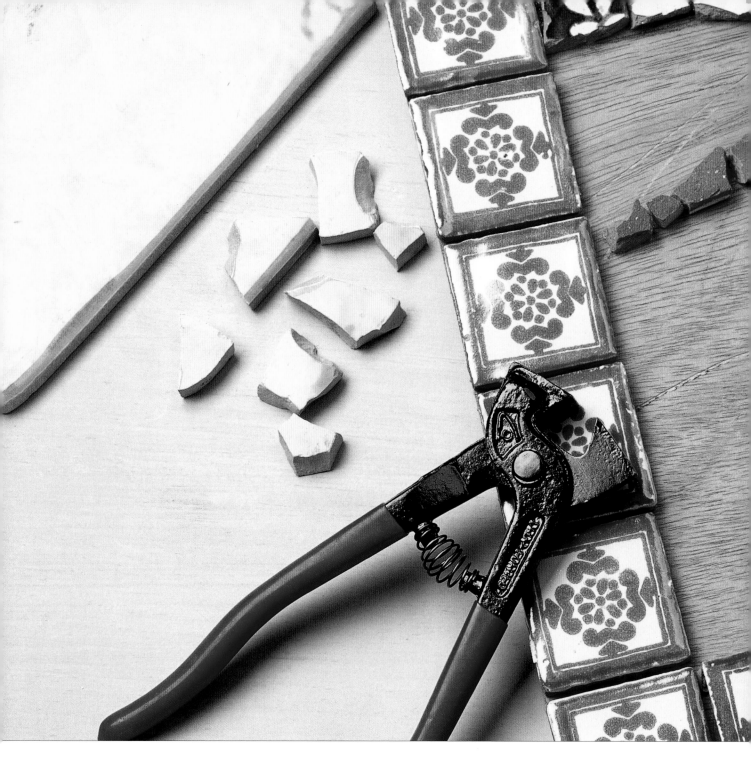

Ceramic Mosaic

Mosaic is a craft achievable by complete beginners. Essentially, it is painting-by-numbers but with miniature tiles, known as tesserae, instead of paint. The skill lies in combining colours together in a pleasing way, and in producing a representative pictorial image. To start with, draw simple stylized shapes freehand or mark out geometric patterns on a plywood base, then fill in the designs with coloured tesserae.

The main materials used in mosaic are the individual pieces, known as tesserae, which can be ceramic, glass, china or any solid material. The other important material to consider is the base, which should be rigid.

Materials

Adhesives

There are several ways of attaching tesserae to a background. Cement-based tile adhesive is the most well known, and it can also be used to grout between the tesserae once the design is complete. For a wood base, use PVA (white) glue. For a glass base, use a silicone-based or a clear, all-purpose adhesive; to stick glass to metal, use epoxy resin. PVA is also used to prime a wooden base to make a suitable surface for the mosaic.

Admix

This is added to tile adhesive for extra adhesion.

Bases

Mosaic can be made on top of almost any rigid and pre-treated surface. One of the most popular bases is plywood.

Brown paper

This is used as backing for mosaics created by the semi-indirect method. Use the heaviest available.

Grout

Specialist grouts are smoother than tile adhesive and are available in a variety of colours.

Shellac

Use this to seal finished mosaics, especially those for outside use.

Tesserae

Mosaic material is described as tesserae. *Ceramic tiles* – These are available in a range of colours and textures, glazed or unglazed. Household tiles can be cut to size using a hammer, or tile nippers for precise shapes.

China – Old china makes unusual tesserae. It creates an uneven surface, so is suitable for decorative projects rather than flat, functional surfaces. Break up china using a hammer.

Marble – Marble can be bought pre-cut into small squares; to cut it with accuracy you need specialist tools.

Mirror glass – Shards of mirror add a reflective sparkle to a mosaic. Mirror can be cut with tile nippers or glass cutters, or broken with a hammer.

Smalti – This is opaque glass that has been cut into regular chunks. It has a softly reflective surface.

Vitreous glass tesserae – These are glass squares which are corrugated on the back to accommodate tile adhesive. They are hardwearing and thus perfect for outdoor projects.

Many of the tools needed to make mosaics are ordinary household equipment; the rest can be purchased in a good hardware store. A pair of tile nippers is the main piece of specialist equipment you will need.

Equipment

Protective goggles
Wear safety goggles when you cut or smash tiles, and when working with hydrochloric acid.

Sacking (heavy cloth)
Use to wrap up tiles before breaking them with a hammer.

Sandpaper
Use coarse-grade sandpaper to prepare wood. To clean finished mosaics, use fine-grade sandpaper and wear a mask.

Saw
Use to cut wooden base material. Use a hacksaw for basic shapes, and a jigsaw for more complicated designs.

Spatula/Spreader/Squeegee
Used for spreading glue or other smooth adhesives, such as cellulose filler, on to your base material.

Tile nippers
These are invaluable for cutting shaped tiles, especially curves.

You will also find the following items useful: bradawl, chalk, craft knife, flexible knife, rubber (latex) gloves, hammer, felt-tipped pen, masking tape, mixing container, nailbrush, paintbrushes, pencil, plastic spray bottle, pliers, ruler, scissors, set square, sponge, tape measure.

Clamps or bench vice
These are needed when cutting out the wooden base for projects.

Dilute hydrochloric acid
Use to clean cement-based grout from the finished mosaic if necessary. Always wear protective clothing, and work in a well-ventilated area.

Drill
A hand electric drill is needed for hanging projects on the wall.

Glass cutter
Use to cut or score glass tesserae.

Paint scraper
This is used to remove awkward pieces of dried tile adhesive or grout from the surface of a completed mosaic.

Protective face mask
You are strongly advised to wear a dust mask when you are mixing powdered grout, sanding the finished mosaic, and cleaning with hydrochloric acid.

Read the instructions below carefully before beginning a mosaic project and choose the methods most appropriate to the design that you are creating. Remember to wear protective gloves and goggles.

Techniques

Cutting tesserae

There are two methods of cutting tesserae, one using tile nippers and one using a hammer. Choose the method depending on the shape of tesserae you require.

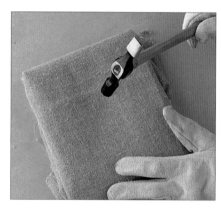

1 Using tile nippers and wearing goggles, hold a tessera or small piece of tile in the tips of the nippers, and squeeze the handles together. It should break along the line of impact. To cut a specific shape, nibble at the edges.

2 Use a hammer to break up larger pieces such as household tiles and china, where regular shapes are not required. Remember to wear goggles to protect your eyes.

3 When working with a hammer it is also advisable to wrap each tile or plate in a piece of sacking or heavy cloth to prevent flying shards.

Drawing a design

Drawing guidelines for your design on the base layer will help you plan your colours and cut your tiles to the right size.

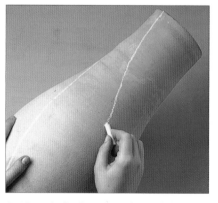

1 Use a soft pencil to sketch a design idea, or to transfer a tracing.

2 Use chalk for a rough guideline on large or awkwardly-shaped bases.

Direct method

This is a popular technique, in which the tesserae are stuck, face up, on to the base and grouted into place. On a three-dimensional object or uneven surface this may be the only suitable method.

1 Cover the base with adhesive and press the tesserae into it. Cover with grout taking care to fill the gaps between the tiles. Remove the excess grout, leave to dry, then clean.

2 If you are following a design drawn on the base as a guide, apply a thin layer of tile adhesive on to the wrong side of each individual tessera and stick it into place.

3 If the tesserae are reflective, such as mirror glass or gold or silver smalti, try placing them at slightly different angles on a three-dimensional surface, to catch the light.

Semi-indirect method

With this method the tesserae are glued to the design off-site, but are then set into the tile adhesive in the final position.

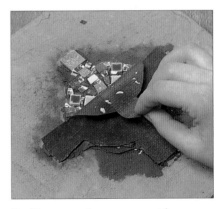

1 Draw a design on to brown paper. Stick the tesserae right side down on to the paper using PVA (white) glue and a brush or palette knife.

2 Spread tile adhesive over the area designated for the mosaic. Press the mosaic into the adhesive, paper side up. Leave to dry for at least 24 hours.

3 Dampen the paper with a wet sponge and peel it off. The mosaic is now ready to be grouted and cleaned.

Indirect method This technique originated as a way of making large mosaics off-site so that they could be transported ready-made. The design is divided into manageable sections which are fitted together on-site.

1 Make a wooden frame to the size required, securing the corners with 2.5cm/1in screws. Make a brown paper template of the inside of the frame. Draw a design on the design area of the paper, leaving a 5mm/¼in margin all around. Grease the inside of the frame with petroleum jelly.

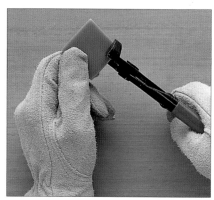

2 Wearing protective goggles and gloves, cut the tesserae as required. Glue them right side down on the brown paper, using water-soluble adhesive and following the design. Leave to dry.

3 Place the wooden frame carefully over the mosaic, then sprinkle dry sand over the mosaic, using a soft brush to spread it into the crevices between the tesserae.

4 Wearing a face mask, on a surface that cannot be damaged, mix 3 parts sand with 1 part cement. Make a well in the centre, add water and mix it with a trowel until you have a firm consistency. Gradually add more water, if necessary, until the mortar is pliable but not runny.

5 Half-fill the frame with mortar, pressing it into the corners. Cut a square of chicken wire a little smaller than the frame. Place it on top of the mortar so that the wire does not touch the frame. Fill the rest of the frame with mortar, then smooth the surface. Cover with damp newspaper, then heavy plastic sheeting, and leave to dry thoroughly for 5–6 days.

6 Turn the frame over. Dampen the brown paper with a wet sponge and then carefully peel it off. Loosen the screws and remove the frame from the mosaic. The mosaic is now ready to be grouted and cleaned.

Grouting

Mosaics are grouted to give them extra strength and a smoother finish. Grout binds the tesserae together. Coloured grout is often used to unify the design; this can either be purchased as ready-made powder, or you can add dye or acrylic paint to plain grout.

1 When grouting three-dimensional objects or uneven surfaces, it is easiest to spread the grout with a flexible knife or spreader.

2 Rub the grout deep into the crevices in between the tesserae. Always wear rubber (latex) gloves when you are handling grout directly.

3 To grout large, flat mosaics, you can use powdered tile adhesive. Spoon it on to the surface, then spread it with a soft brush to fill all the crevices between the tesserae.

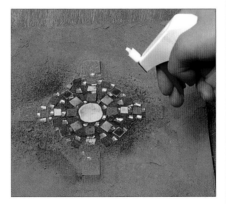

4 When you have completed the grouting process, spray the adhesive with water from a plastic spray bottle. You may need to repeat the process to achieve a smooth finish.

Cleaning

It is best to remove excess grout while it is still wet. Scrub from the surface using a strong, stiff-bristled nailbrush and then polish-off.

Cement mortars and cement-based adhesives need rougher treatment, and you will probably need to use sandpaper. A quick and fast alternative is to dilute hydrochloric acid and then paint it on to the surface to dissolve the excess cement. The process should be done outside, as it gives off toxic fumes. When the excess cement has fizzed away, wash off the residue of acid from the mosaic with plenty of water. Remember to wear a face mask when sanding, and a face mask, goggles and gloves when using hydrochloric acid.

Fragments of plain and patterned broken tile have been worked into the design of these plant pots. Collect materials by looking in second-hand shops for old china in contrasting and complementary patterns.

Plant Pots

You will need

terracotta flower pots

PVA (white) glue and brush (optional)

mixing container

acrylic paint

paintbrush

chalk or wax crayon

plain and patterned ceramic tiles

tile nippers

rubber (latex) gloves

flexible knife

tile adhesive

powdered waterproof tile grout

cement dye

cloth

nailbrush

lint-free, soft cloth

1 If the pots are not frost-resistant and they are intended for outdoor use, treat inside and out by sealing with a coat of diluted PVA (white) glue. Allow to dry. Paint the inside of all the pots with acrylic paint in your chosen colour. Leave to dry. Using chalk or a wax crayon, roughly sketch out the design for the tile pieces.

2 Snip small pieces of ceramic tile to fit within your chosen design. Using a flexible knife, spread tile adhesive on to small areas of the design at a time. Press the tile pieces in place, working on the outlines first, and then filling in the background.

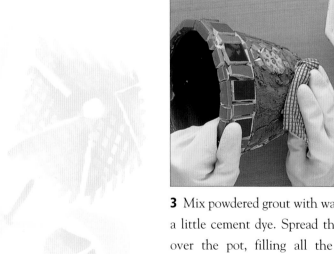

3 Mix powdered grout with water and a little cement dye. Spread the grout over the pot, filling all the cracks between the tile pieces. Allow the surface to dry thoroughly.

4 Brush off any excess with a nailbrush. Allow to dry thoroughly for at least 48 hours, and then polish with a dry, soft cloth.

This delicate mosaic is made entirely from old cups and plates. The pretty trinket box is ideal for displaying on a dressing table, and can be used for storing jewellery, letters and other treasures.

Floral Trinket Box

You will need
wooden box
PVA (white) glue
mixing container
old household paintbrush
bradawl or other sharp instrument
soft dark pencil
tile nippers
white and patterned old china
cement-based tile adhesive
admix
flexible knife
cloths
paint scraper

1 Prime the top and sides of the wooden box with diluted PVA (white) glue. Leave to dry, then score it at random with a bradawl or other sharp implement to key the surface.

2 Using a soft pencil and the template at the back of the book, draw a grid on the box. Draw a flower in each square, with a large flower in the centre.

3 Cut the pieces of white china into small squares. Mix the tile adhesive with admix. Using a flexible knife, spread this along the grid lines, a small area at a time.

4 Press the white tesserae into the adhesive in neat, close-fitting rows. Cover all of the grid lines on the top and sides of the box. Leave it to dry completely overnight.

5 Using tile nippers, cut out small pieces of the patterned china. Sort them into colours. Position the tesserae on the box and plan out the colour scheme.

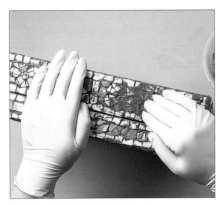

6 Spread the tile adhesive and admix over each square of the top and sides in turn. Press in the tesserae to make each flower and the background. Leave to dry.

7 Spread tile adhesive all over the surface of the mosaic, getting right into the crevices and wiping off excess adhesive with a damp cloth.

8 Using a flexible knife, smooth the tile adhesive around the hinges and clasp, if there is one. Remove any excess adhesive immediately with a cloth before it dries. Leave to dry.

9 Using a paint scraper, scrape off any tile adhesive that may have dried on the surface of the mosaic. Take care not to scratch the surface of the tiles.

10 When all the excess grout has been removed, polish the surface of the box with a soft cloth, rubbing each tile fragment to a high shine.

Sometimes simple designs are the most striking, and this one certainly doesn't demand any artistic skill. Choose a vase with an elegant shape, and use whatever colours you like, to match the decor of your room.

Spiral Vase

You will need

tall vase

paintbrush (optional)

yacht varnish (optional)

white chalk

marble tile

piece of sacking (heavy cloth)

hammer

cement-based tile adhesive

mixing container

flexible knife

pale blue and royal blue, glazed ceramic tiles

gold smalti

tile nippers

notched spreader or cloth pad

sandpaper

soft cloth

1 If your vase is unglazed, seal it by painting all around the inside top lip with yacht varnish. Using a piece of white chalk, draw lines spiralling gently from the rim of the vase to the base. Make sure you have an even number of bands and that they are regularly spaced.

2 Wrap the marble tile in sacking (heavy cloth), then break it up using a hammer. Mix up the tile adhesive following the manufacturer's instructions. Using a flexible knife, spread a thin band around the top and bottom of the vase, press in the marble pieces and leave to dry overnight.

3 Using a hammer and sacking, break up all the pale blue and royal blue tiles. Spread tile adhesive over the vase, a band at a time, and press in the tesserae, alternating the two colours. Leave to dry, preferably overnight.

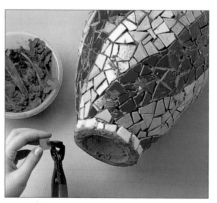

4 Use the tile nippers to cut the gold smalti into small pieces. Using the knife, place blobs of adhesive in the larger gaps between the blue tesserae. Press the gold smalti pieces at random over the blue spirals, checking that they are all level with the rest of the tiles. Leave to dry overnight.

5 Using a notched spreader or cloth pad, rub more tile adhesive in the colour of your choice, over the surface of the mosaic, carefully filling all the gaps. Wipe off the excess and leave to dry overnight. Sand off any adhesive dried on the surface, then polish with a clean, soft cloth.

The daisy-filled panels of this pine bedhead would look beautiful in a country bedroom with distressed wooden furniture. Make a footboard to match or use the same design to decorate other panelled furniture.

Mosaic Bedhead

You will need

unvarnished pine bedhead and footboard
PVA (white) glue and brush
craft knife
old palette knife or flexible spreader
cement-based tile adhesive
admix
mixing container
soft pencil
plain, glazed ceramic tiles: white, orange, green and honey-coloured
piece of heavy sacking
hammer
tile nippers
rubber-edged spreader
lint-free cloth
sponge
sanding block

1 Seal the surface of the wood with PVA (white) glue. When dry, score the surface with a craft knife.

2 Using a palette knife or flexible spreader, fill any recesses in the areas to be decorated with the tile adhesive mixed with admix. Leave for 24 hours to allow the adhesive to set.

4 Wrap each white and orange tile separately in sacking and break them with a hammer. Trim the white tile pieces into petal shapes with the tile nippers. Trim the orange tile pieces into round centres for the daisies.

5 Spread tile adhesive over the daisy shapes on the panels. Press the white and orange mosaic pieces in place to make flowers.

3 Draw a daisy design on the panels with a soft pencil.

6 Smash the green tiles as before and shape the pieces with tile nippers to make stems and leaves. Spread the adhesive over the appropriate areas of the design, then press the green mosaic pieces into position.

7 Make all the leaves and stems, and then leave the tile adhesive to dry for 24 hours.

8 Smash the honey-coloured tiles as before. Spread tile adhesive around the daisies and fill in the background, cutting the pieces of tile as necessary so that they fit.

9 Using a rubber-edged spreader or lint-free cloth, spread adhesive over the mosaic, pushing it into the gaps and covering all the sharp corners. Remove excess with a damp sponge.

10 Leave the mosaic for 24 hours to dry, then lightly smooth the surface of the mosaic with a sanding block. Polish with a dry, lint-free cloth.

Templates

Enlarge the templates on a photocopier. Alternatively, trace the design and draw a grid of evenly spaced squares over your tracing. Draw a larger grid on to another piece of paper and copy the outline square by square. Finally, draw over the lines to make sure they are continuous.

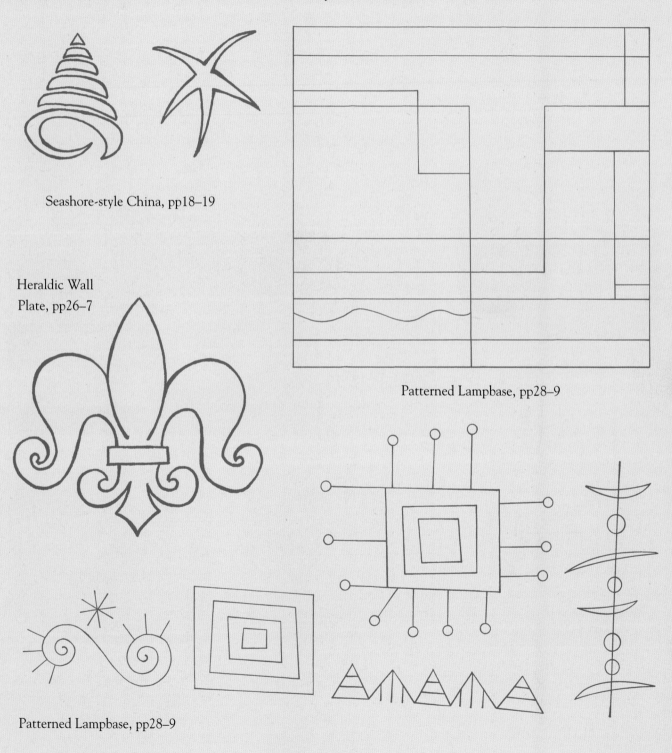

Seashore-style China, pp18–19

Heraldic Wall
Plate, pp26–7

Patterned Lampbase, pp28–9

Patterned Lampbase, pp28–9

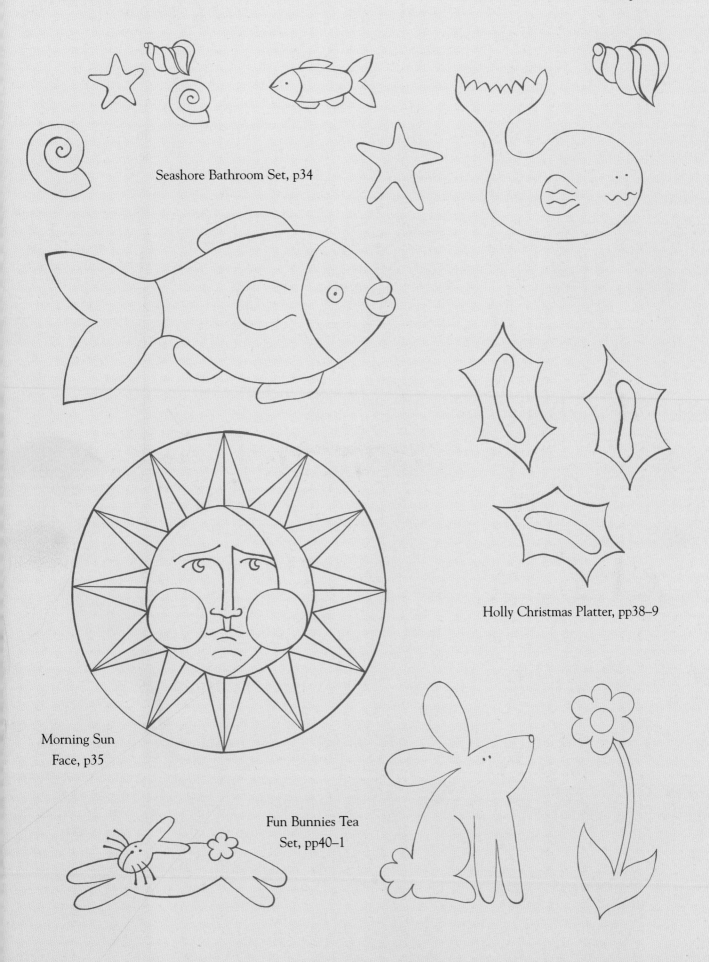

Seashore Bathroom Set, p34

Holly Christmas Platter, pp38–9

Morning Sun
Face, p35

Fun Bunnies Tea
Set, pp40–1

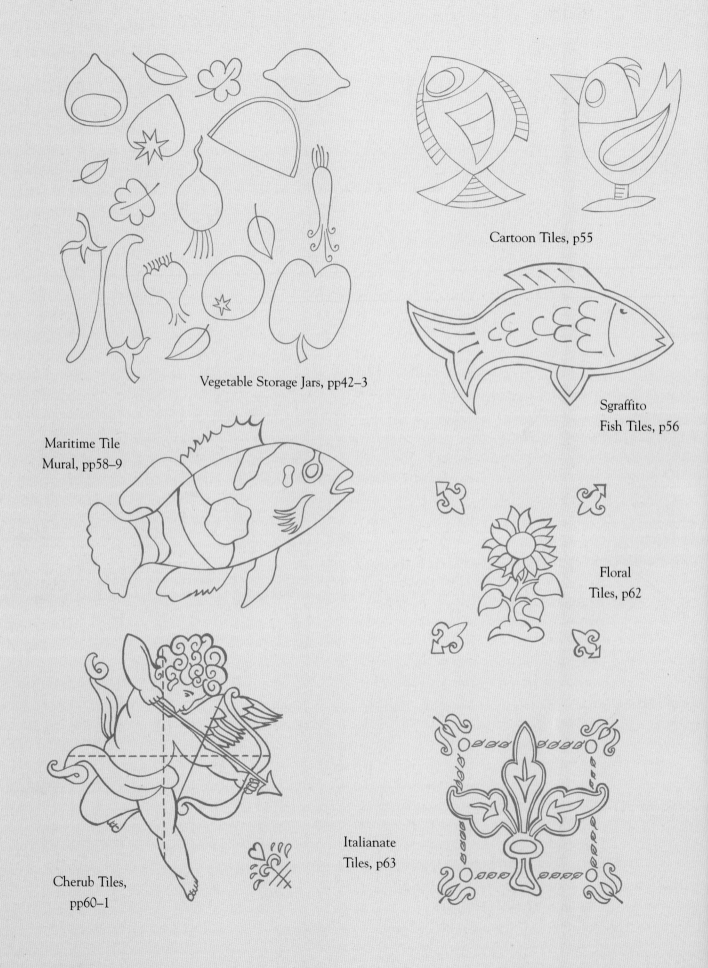

Cartoon Tiles, p55

Vegetable Storage Jars, pp42–3

Sgraffito
Fish Tiles, p56

Maritime Tile
Mural, pp58–9

Floral
Tiles, p62

Cherub Tiles,
pp60–1

Italianate
Tiles, p63

Art Nouveau Tiles, pp68–9

Majolica Tile, p64

Byzantine Bird Tile, p65

William Morris Tiles, pp74–5

Floral Trinket Box, pp86–7

Index